cooking
Italian
with kids

Liz Franklin
photography by Lisa Linder

cooking
Italian
with **kids**

RYLAND
PETERS
&SMALL
LONDON NEW YORK

Senior designer Megan Smith
Senior editor Céline Hughes
Location & model research
  Emily Westlake
Production manager
  Patricia Harrington
Art director Leslie Harrington
Publishing director Alison Starling

Food stylist Joy Skipper
Prop stylist Liz Belton
Indexer Sandra Shotter

First published in the
United Kingdom in 2008 by
Ryland Peters and Small
20–21 Jockey's Fields
London WC1R 4BW

www.rylandpeters.com

10 9 8 7 6 5 4 3 2 1

Text © Liz Franklin 2008
Design and photographs
© Ryland Peters & Small 2008

ISBN: 978-1-84597-703-0

• All fruit and vegetables should
be thoroughly washed before eating
or cooking.

• All spoon measurements are level,
unless otherwise specified.

• Ovens should be preheated to
the specified temperature. Recipes
in this book were tested using a
regular oven. If using a fan-assisted
oven, follow the manufacturer's
instructions for adjusting
temperatures.

• All eggs are medium, unless
otherwise specified. Recipes
containing raw or partially cooked
egg, or raw fish or shellfish, should
not be served to the very young, very
old, anyone with a compromised
immune system or pregnant women.

contents

buon appetito!

'A tavola!' is a familiar and happy cry in houses all over Italy at mealtimes: it's the call for everyone to drop what they're doing and come to the table to eat, whether for a simple lunch or a sumptuous feast.

From the humblest means all the way up to aristocracy, Italians have a very special attitude to food; eating is not about simply refuelling or self-indulgence, but about sitting down together around the table and enjoying the companionship of others. Mealtimes are a time for family and friends to meet en masse, to enjoy lovely food, chat and delight in each other's company, listen to each other's news and reflect on one another's day.

Despite the hustle and bustle of the rush-around lives we seem to live now, when it comes to food, the Italians still seem to have their priorities firmly set. Generally speaking, neither the preparation of food nor the eating

of it is a hurried affair – although naturally in the 21st century there are always exceptions! This means that, for the most part, Italian children grow up from an early age with a love of good food; they also develop discerning palates, get to know about ingredients, learn about table manners and, often as an added bonus, discover the art of conversation too! All of these are important factors to those of us concerned about the damage that junk food and eating on the hoof are doing to our health and social skills.

In Italy particularly, cooking is rarely considered a chore, but rather an act of love. Passing down beloved kitchen secrets and recipes through generations is something that still goes on, and doing so is all part of the native passion for good food. Mamma's and Nonna's (Grandma's) recipes are usually considered the best by their loyal descendants and looked upon as precious treasure!

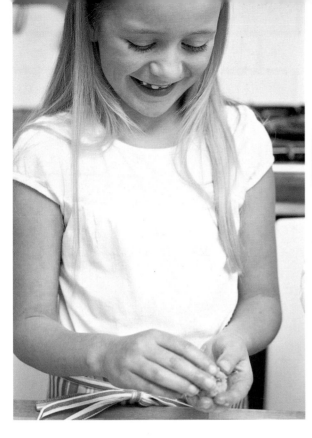

For children, helping in the kitchen is always an exciting thing to do – all those fabulous ingredients to chop and stir; the enticing smells; the textures and colours; the little nibbles and tastes along the way. And at the end of it, the very special feeling when they proudly show off their efforts to family and friends and see the delight as everyone tucks into the fruits of their labours. Imagine then how full of pride the youngsters in your life will be if the recipes are actually aimed at them and you are merely the one helping out with the tricky bits and the hot spots (plus the shopping before and the washing-up after!)

This book is packed with delicious Italian recipes that I have shared with my own three sons, Chris, Oliver and Tim. All four of us have always had a great passion for Italian food, and now we are lucky enough to have a house there, every day seems to bring new and delicious discoveries.

Some of the recipes that follow are based on dishes we've eaten in restaurants or cafés, or bought in pastry shops or even supermarkets. Some are influenced by classics, while others are borrowed from our Italian friends and tweaked the tiniest bit to take into account the difference in available ingredients outside Italy. I've tried to offer simple, child-friendly family recipes rather than those that will appeal only to young appetites, thereby encouraging the whole extended family to join in and appreciate the pleasure that home-cooked food can bring.

In a truly Italian way, some of the recipes in this book are full of goodness and the freshest ingredients, and others are meant to be occasional treats for those with a sweet tooth. I hope you enjoy sharing them with your children, and who knows, maybe they will carry some of them along through life and in time pass them on to their children too.

italian essentials

EXTRA VIRGIN OLIVE OIL (OLIO EXTRA VERGINE DI OLIVA)

There are lots of kinds of olive oil, but the best and healthiest is extra virgin olive oil. I always use this type in all my cooking – sometimes I even make cakes with it! You don't have to use an expensive one for cooking; a supermarket own brand should be good enough as long as it is labelled extra virgin. You could pay a little more for a special one to drizzle on salads though. Always use extra virgin in the recipes in this book.

BASIL (BASILICO)

Basil has such a sunny, cheery smell; it always reminds me of Italy, perhaps because it goes so well in delicious tomato sauces and salads, on pizza and with pasta. Make sure you use only the freshest basil with perky green leaves – no black, droopy bits! You can easily grow it in pots on a sunny windowsill in the summer. For the best results, always add it to dishes at the last minute, and don't chop it, as you will lose some of the flavour. Tear it instead – it's less fussy that way anyway.

BAY LEAVES (ALLORO)

Bay leaves find their way into a lot of dishes in Italian cooking. They add a lovely subtle flavour to pasta sauces, soups and casseroles, and I add them to milky puddings too. Fresh bay leaves are good, but you can dry the leaves whole and simply pop them in a screw-topped jar.

OREGANO (ORIGANO)

Fresh oregano isn't always easy to find, but it dries well, so it's a good idea to keep a jar in the cupboard for tomato-based sauces and to scatter over pizza when you can't get hold of fresh basil. If you're buying it in the supermarket's dried herbs and spices section, try to find the freeze-dried kind, which has a much better flavour.

PARSLEY (PREZZEMOLO)

Italian parsley is the flat-leafed kind rather than the very frilly kind usually known as curly parsley. Parsley is probably used in Italian cooking even more than basil is – in all kinds of soups, stews and sauces. You can grow it in a pot on a windowsill; you can even freeze fresh parsley and crumble it straight from the freezer into sauces and such as you need it.

ROSEMARY (ROSMARINO)

Rosemary is another herb that is used a lot in Italian cooking; it's used to flavour roast meats and vegetables. It makes a fantastic flavouring for focaccia too – see the recipe on page 30. Always try to use fresh rosemary, as dried isn't really very nice at all.

SAGE (SALVIA)

Sage is another well-loved herb in Italian dishes and it's especially lovely with pork. It's also ultra delicious with pumpkin belly button pasta parcels, as I hope you will agree when you try the recipe on page 26!

PARMESAN CHEESE (PARMIGIANO REGGIANO)

Real Italian Parmesan cheese is a very special cheese indeed; it is also called Parmigiano Reggiano and carries a special official certificate to prove that it has passed very strict standards and been produced only in certain areas. It is known as the King of Italian Cheeses and is fabulous grated over soups and pasta, shaved onto salads or stirred into risottos – but do buy a whole piece and grate it as you need it because ready-grated Parmesan just doesn't have the same flavour.

PANCETTA (PANCETTA)

Pancetta is a type of Italian bacon; it comes in whole pieces, or little matchstick pieces called lardons. You can buy it easily in supermarkets and delis. It is used in sauces and casseroles.

GARLIC (AGLIO)

Garlic isn't a particularly Italian ingredient but many of the recipes in Italian cuisine wouldn't be the same without it. Don't worry, Italian dishes don't often taste very strongly of garlic – it's used to help add a subtle flavour. Be careful not to fry it at high temperatures, as it turns bitter and yucky if it gets too brown.

TOMATOES (POMODORI)

It's difficult to imagine Italian food without thinking about tomatoes. In Italy there are some wonderful varieties and they come in all shapes and sizes – it's often the funny-looking ones that taste the best! At home, choose plump, juicy ripe tomatoes in the summer, but in the winter months it can often be best to use good-quality tinned tomatoes. I love using the little cherry ones you can buy in tins now – they have a lovely sweet flavour and make the most delicious sauce.

SETTING A PRETTY TABLE

There's nothing especially Italian about setting a pretty table at which to eat, but it makes everyone feel good if they are in pleasant surroundings. You may like to lay a tablecloth, place mats and napkins – mats will protect the table and napkins always come in handy for wiping mouths and hands when you've been slurping spaghetti or tucking into a big slice of pizza! For special meals, you might like to add a few flowers. You don't need to go to the trouble of using a fancy vase – a simple drinking glass can look just as good.

KITCHEN EQUIPMENT

You are likely to have most of the kitchen equipment needed to prepare and cook all the recipes in your kitchen at home already; weighing scales, mixing bowls, wooden spoons, chopping boards, knives, whisks, a rolling pin, pastry cutters (although you can use an upturned glass), saucepans, cake tins, baking trays etc. If you wanted to treat yourself to a pasta maker or an ice-cream maker, they are great tools for any budding Italian chef to have and they aren't too expensive. Of course, you can make the pasta and ice cream without them, but they do make life a little easier if you love pasta and ice cream as much as we do in our house.

People seem to love pasta the world over, but as you would expect, none so much as the Italians. The Italians eat pasta every day – and I do mean every day. I used to be amazed when I looked inside other people's trolleys at my local supermarket in Italy; most of them seemed to include not two or three packets of pasta, as you might imagine, but probably nearer a dozen and sometimes more! 90 per cent of Italians eat dried pasta, the most popular brand being De Cecco, and every trolley I saw seemed to have a little mountain of the familiar blue and yellow packets. I saw an assortment of spaghetti, linguine, penne, farfalle, fusilli, cavatappi – swirls, curls, strands, tubes and bows. Different shapes for different sauces: chunky shapes and wide ribbons for rich, meaty sauces; fine lengths and thin strands for delicate sauces.

Pasta is quick to cook and healthy too (as long as you don't eat your way through mountains of it and sit around on your bottom afterwards!) Marathon runners eat lots of pasta. During the children's cookery classes I used to run, the children loved to make fresh pasta. I used to giggle and chant at the start of the class 'pasta, pasta, makes you go faster'.

pasta

This is possibly the most important – and simplest – Italian recipe you'll ever need. Master this and there will be a world of scrumptious meals at your fingertips!

basic egg pasta

300 g Italian type 'oo' flour,
plus extra to sprinkle
a pinch of salt
3 eggs
a pasta machine (optional)

Serves 4

1 Sift the flour and salt into a large bowl. Make a well in the centre and add the eggs. If you like, you can use a food processor instead – just **ask an adult to help you** put the flour, salt and eggs in the bowl of the food processor ready for mixing.

2 Bring the mixture together by mixing the ingredients with your fingertips, or press the 'pulse' button on the food processor repeatedly to make the ingredients combine. You should have a soft but not sticky dough.

3 Sprinkle a little flour on a clean work surface, turn the dough out onto it and knead (see Tip on the next page) for 4–5 minutes. Wrap the dough in clingfilm and put it in the fridge for at least 30 minutes before using.

4 If you have a pasta machine, set the lasagne rollers to the widest setting. Take a quarter of the pasta dough out of the fridge and keep the remaining dough wrapped in clingfilm.

5 Flatten your small lump of dough until it fits through the rollers of the machine. **Ask an adult to help you** flatten the dough by passing it through the machine.

6 Take the flattened dough and fold it into 3. Run it through the machine again and then fold it into 3 once more. Repeat this process another 3 times, so that the dough has gone through the machine on the same setting a total of five times. The dough should be nice and smooth and pliable.

7 Reduce the roller width by one notch and pass the pasta through again.

8 Repeat the process, reducing the roller width by one notch each time. You may have to cut the pasta sheet in half to fit into the machine. If you do, remember to keep the dough you are not working with covered with clingfilm because it will become too dry to work with if it is left exposed to the air for too long.

9 Once the dough has been through the smallest roller width, you can then make spaghetti, tagliatelle or pappardelle by passing your sheet of pasta through the right settings of your machine (follow the instructions in the manual), or you can ask an adult to help you cut the pasta sheets with a knife. Alternatively, you can use the sheets to make lasagne, ravioli (page 24) or belly button pasta parcels (page 26).

10 If you don't have a pasta machine, you will need to sprinkle a little flour on a clean work surface and roll out the dough with a rolling pin. It will take some effort and strength to get the dough super-thin, but keep at it! It may be easier for you to roll out a quarter of the dough at a time (remember to keep the remaining dough wrapped in clingfilm so that it doesn't dry out).

TIP To knead dough, push the heels of your hands into the lump of dough and squash down. Swivel the dough around slightly and squash down again. Keep swivelling and turning the dough over so that you are kneading it evenly all over. If it gets too flat, fold the dough over onto itself to make it into a lump again and keep kneading. It's hard work, but it's worth it – when you've finished you'll have a firm, smooth, gorgeously stretchy dough!

This is a lovely easy sauce that bubbles away to become deliciously sticky. It's a little like spaghetti Bolognese.

tagliatelle with rich meat sauce
tagliatelle con sugo di carne

1 recipe tagliatelle (page 12)
   or 400 g shop-bought
   dried tagliatelle
salt and black pepper
freshly grated Parmesan,
   to serve

For the sauce
1 onion
1 carrot
2 garlic cloves
1 celery stick
3 tablespoons olive oil
450 g lean minced beef
400-g tin cherry tomatoes
   (or regular chopped)
300 ml beef stock
1 teaspoon caster sugar
1 teaspoon mixed dried
   herbs

Serves 4

1 To make the sauce, **ask an adult to help you** peel the onion and carrot and chop them finely. Peel the garlic cloves (see Tip on page 18) and crush them with a garlic crusher. Trim the ends of the celery and pull off some of the nasty stringy bits from the outside. Chop the celery finely.

2 **Ask an adult to help you** heat the olive oil in a saucepan and fry the onion, carrot, garlic and celery over gentle heat for 5–6 minutes, until everything is soft but not coloured.

3 Add the minced beef to the saucepan and break it up into pieces with a wooden spoon. Leave it to cook for 5 minutes, stirring occasionally, until it has turned brown all over.

4 Stir in the tinned tomatoes, stock, sugar and mixed herbs, then season with a little sea salt and freshly ground black pepper. Leave the sauce to bubble for about 25 minutes, until it has reduced and is glossy and thick.

5 In the meantime, **ask an adult to help you** cook the tagliatelle. Bring a big saucepan of water to the boil and add a pinch of salt. Drop in the tagliatelle and cook for about 2 minutes if you've made it fresh, or according to the instructions on the packet if you bought it dried, from a shop. The tagliatelle is ready when it is 'al dente' (see Tip below).

6 Drain the pasta and toss with the sauce. Serve at once with freshly grated Parmesan.

TIP To check if pasta is perfectly cooked, **ask an adult to help you** fish out a strand of tagliatelle (or whatever type of pasta you are cooking) from the hot water, blow on it till it's cool enough to eat, then carefully take a bite. The pasta should be soft but not soggy, and should still retain a little bite to it. When it's cooked like this, it's called 'al dente'!

This is the simplest of pasta dishes; but the simplest food can often be the most magical. If you like chillies, there is a similar dish to this that includes a couple of chopped chillies or a pinch of chilli flakes with the garlic-infused olive oil. Never be afraid to experiment – that's how we discover new things!

spaghetti with herbs & garlic
spaghetti alle erbe e aglio

1 recipe spaghetti (page 12) or 400 g shop-bought dried spaghetti
a pinch of salt
1 unwaxed lemon
a large handful of mixed fresh herbs (such as chives, parsley and basil), leaves torn
100 ml olive oil
3 garlic cloves
freshly grated Parmesan, to serve

Serves 4

1 **Ask an adult to help you** cook the spaghetti. Bring a big saucepan of water to the boil and add the salt. Drop in the spaghetti and cook it for about 2 minutes if you've made it fresh, or according to the instructions on the packet if you bought it dried, from a shop. The spaghetti is ready when it is 'al dente' (see Tip on page 14).

2 Wash the lemon and **ask an adult to help you** grate the zest (see Tip on page 24).

3 While the spaghetti is cooking, **ask an adult to help you** heat the oil in a frying pan over medium heat.

4 Peel the garlic cloves (see Tip below). Add the whole cloves to the frying pan and leave to warm and infuse the oil for 3–4 minutes.

5 **Ask an adult to help you** fish the garlic out of the oil with a slotted spoon.

6 Drain the pasta and toss with the infused oil, the lemon zest and the herbs. Serve at once with freshly grated Parmesan.

TIP It can be fiddly to peel a garlic clove as the skin tends to stick to the garlic. Here's an easy trick: put the clove flat on a chopping board. Take a wide, blunt knife and place it, flat-side down, on top of the clove and push down hard with your hand. This loosens the skin and makes peeling much quicker!

Bread is the foundation of the Italian diet, so much so that Italians generally buy fresh bread everyday and it is the first thing to go on the lunch or dinner table. Even the smallest villages still have bakeries, and there you can usually find a selection of... varies throughout Italy from region to region.

In some... it is not unusual for people to bake at home... however... aren't so lucky and local bakeries are...

...home can be great fun and satisfying.

...a grain that has become very... ...of the 1900s when... a fresh... ...was a staple of the Italian diet.

Polenta... smooth to fill you up...

...rough tending... teamed with... ...immediately. Traditionally, it was very slow to prepare... ...readily available in supermarkets... ...up in honour of the idea of using them... ...I encourage you to use them.

bread & polenta

This heavenly bread is so delicious and satisfying – and easy too!

rosemary focaccia
focaccia con rosmarino

6 tablespoons olive oil

a large bunch of fresh rosemary, leaves only

500 g strong bread flour, plus extra to sprinkle

1 sachet (7 g) fast action dried yeast

1 teaspoon salt

about 200 ml warm water (see Tip below right)

rock salt

a baking tray, about 20 x 30 cm, dusted with flour

Makes one loaf

1 Put the olive oil and rosemary into a bowl. Squeeze the rosemary with your hands to infuse the oil.

2 Put the flour, yeast and salt into a bowl and stir well. Stir in 2 tablespoons of the rosemary-infused olive oil and 1–2 tablespoons warm water. Put your hands right in the bowl and mix the ingredients with your fingers. Keep adding warm water, a little at a time, until you get a soft but not sticky dough.

3 Sprinkle a little flour over a clean work surface, turn the dough out onto it and knead for 5–10 minutes (see Tip on page 13). The dough should be very smooth and pliable.

4 Using a rolling pin, roll the dough out into a rectangle slightly smaller than the prepared baking tray. Lift it carefully into the tray, cover the tray with a clean tea towel and leave it to rise in a warm place for about 1 hour, until the dough is double the original size.

5 **Ask an adult to help you** preheat the oven to 200°C (400°F) Gas 6.

6 Uncover the dough, which should be almost bursting out of the tray by now! Push your thumb all over it (don't worry if this deflates it) to make big dimples. Scatter some rock salt over the top.

7 **Ask an adult to help you** put the bread in the preheated oven and bake for about 20–25 minutes. **Ask an adult to help you** test the bread – it should be firm and golden and sound hollow when tapped on its bottom!

8 Leave to cool on a wire rack and serve cut into squares.

TIP The warm water used to make bread dough should be about as warm as your hands. So if you put your fingers in a bowl of the water, it should feel nice and warm – neither too hot nor too cold.

These mini-focaccias taste fantastic all on their own, although you could fill them to make sandwiches too. They make great picnic or lunchbox food.

mini-focaccias with courgettes
focaccine alle zucchine

400 g strong bread flour
1 sachet (7 g) fast action
   dried yeast
3 tablespoons olive oil
about 200 ml warm water
   (see Tip on page 30)
2 small courgettes
salt
2 large baking trays,
   dusted with flour

Makes 8

1 Put the flour, yeast and 1 teaspoon salt into a bowl and stir well. Stir in just 2 tablespoons of the olive oil and 1–2 tablespoons warm water. Put your hands right in the bowl and mix the ingredients with your fingers. Keep adding warm water, a little at a time, until you get a soft but not sticky dough.

2 Sprinkle a little flour over a clean work surface, turn the dough out onto it and knead for 5–10 minutes (see Tip on page 13). The dough should be very smooth and pliable.

3 Divide the dough into 8 pieces and knead each piece again until smooth. Using a rolling pin, roll each piece into small circles just over 1 cm thick. Lay the circles, spaced well apart, on the prepared baking trays and leave to rise in a warm place for about 40 minutes, until double their original size.

4 **Ask an adult to help you** preheat the oven to 220°C (425°F) Gas 7.

5 **Ask an adult to help you** top and tail the courgettes and grate them carefully into a bowl with a cheese grater. Season with a little salt. Add the remaining olive oil and toss well with your hands.

6 Scatter the grated courgettes over the mini-focaccias.

7 **Ask an adult to help you** put the bread into the preheated oven and bake for about 10–15 minutes. **Ask an adult to help you** test them – they should be firm and golden, and sound hollow when tapped on their bottoms!

8 Serve warm, or leave to cool on a wire rack.

little cheese & tomato pizzas
pizzette margherita

200 g mozzarella
salt and black pepper

For the sauce
1 onion
2 garlic cloves
3 tablespoons olive oil
400-g tin cherry tomatoes
2 teaspoons caster sugar
a small handful of fresh basil

For the bases
500 g strong bread flour, plus extra to sprinkle
1 sachet (7 g) fast action dried yeast
1 tablespoon olive oil
200 ml warm water (see Tip on page 30)
2 large baking trays, dusted with flour

Makes 6

1 Ask an adult to help you make the sauce. Peel the onion and chop it finely. Peel the garlic cloves (see Tip on page 18) and crush them with a garlic crusher. Heat the olive oil in a saucepan and fry the onion and garlic over gentle heat for about 4–5 minutes, until everything is soft but not coloured.

2 Add the tinned tomatoes and sugar, then season with a little salt and black pepper. Leave the sauce to bubble for 10–15 minutes, until glossy and thick, then add the basil and leave the mixture to simmer gently for 5 minutes more. Remove from the heat and set aside.

3 In the meantime, **ask an adult to help you** preheat the oven to 220° C (425°F) Gas 7.

4 To make the bases, put the flour, yeast and a pinch of salt into a bowl and stir well.

5 Stir in the olive oil and 1–2 tablespoons warm water. Put your hands right in the bowl and mix the ingredients with your fingers. Keep adding warm water, a little at a time, until you get a soft but not sticky dough.

6 Sprinkle a little flour over a clean work surface, turn the dough out onto it and knead for 5–10 minutes (see Tip on page 13). The dough should be very smooth and pliable.

7 Divide the dough into 6 pieces. Using a rolling pin, roll each piece into a circle about 10 cm in diameter and lay them on the prepared baking trays. Spread a thin layer of tomato sauce on each pizza base.

8 Break the mozzarella into small nuggets and dot them evenly over the pizza bases.

9 Ask an adult to help you put the tray into the oven. Bake the pizzas for 6–7 minutes, until the bases are golden and the cheese is bubbling. Serve at once.

Pizzette – little pizzas – are a favourite snack all over Italy, and you can buy them freshly made from the baker to eat on the go. They're not so easy to find outside Italy, but the good news is that they're a doddle to make at home!

Italy is shaped like a big, long boot which looks like it's kicking a ball. The 'ball' is a beautiful island called Sardinia where they make this crunchy parchment bread. It's so thin that it looks like a sheet of music, hence the Italian name 'carta di musica'. Not only is it delicious, it's also fun to make because it doesn't need yeast and so it doesn't have to be left to rise like most breads. You need to roll the dough so thinly that you can almost see through it – or, if you don't mind having long pieces instead of circles, you could cheat a little and put it through a pasta machine. Make sure an adult is on hand to turn the bread halfway through the cooking – a pair of tongs is useful for this.

crunchy sardinian parchment bread
carta di musica

280 g plain flour, plus extra to sprinkle
160 g fine semolina
1 teaspoon salt
1½ tablespoons finely chopped fresh rosemary
300 ml warm water (see Tip on page 30)
2 large baking trays, dusted with flour

Makes 10-12

1 **Ask an adult to help you** preheat the oven to 220°C (425°F) Gas 7.

2 Put the flour, semolina, salt and rosemary into a bowl and mix thoroughly.

3 Pour in 1–2 tablespoons warm water. Put your hands right in the bowl and mix the ingredients with your fingers. Keep adding warm water, a little at a time, until you get a soft but not sticky dough.

4 Sprinkle a little flour over a clean work surface, turn the dough out onto it and knead for 2–3 minutes (see Tip on page 13). The dough should be very smooth and pliable.

5 Divide the dough into 10–12 pieces. Using a rolling pin, roll each piece out into large, roughly shaped wafer-thin circles.

6 Lay the circles on the prepared baking trays (you will have to cook the bread in several batches). **Ask an adult to help you** put the bread in the oven and bake for 2–3 minutes, until golden and puffy. Make sure the adult is the one to carefully turn the bread over. Cook it for a further 2 minutes. **Ask the adult to help you** remove the trays from the oven. When the tray and the bread have cooled, remove the bread and store in an airtight tin until you are ready to eat it.

This is a lovely treat for breakfast and makes good use of fabulous summer plums. Choose plums which are sweet but not too squidgy, or they will ooze and make the bread soggy.

sweet plum focaccia

focaccia dolce con le prugne

450 g Italian type 'oo' flour,
    plus extra to sprinkle
1 sachet (7 g) fast action
    dried yeast
a pinch of salt
80 g caster sugar
60 g butter
about 200 ml warm water
    (see Tip on page 30)

For the topping
3–4 ripe but firm plums
1 tablespoon caster sugar
*a rectangular baking tray,
    20 x 30 cm, dusted with
    flour*

Makes one loaf

1 Put the flour, yeast, salt and sugar into a bowl and stir well.

2 **Ask an adult to help you** melt the butter in a small saucepan.

3 Stir the melted butter into the bowl with the flour mixture. Pour in 1–2 tablespoons warm water. Put your hands right in the bowl and mix the ingredients with your fingers. Keep adding warm water, a little at a time, until you get a soft but not sticky dough.

4 Sprinkle a little flour over a clean work surface, turn the dough out onto it and knead for 5–10 minutes (see Tip on page 13). The dough should be very smooth and pliable.

5 Using a rolling pin, roll the dough out into a rectangle slightly smaller than the prepared baking tray. Lift it carefully into the tray, cover with a clean tea towel and leave it to rise in a

warm place (like the airing cupboard!) until the dough is double the original size.

6 **Ask an adult to help you** preheat the oven to 200°C (400°F) Gas 6.

7 **Ask an adult to help you** slice the plums in half and remove the stones. Cut the plums into thin slices and dab them on some kitchen paper to remove any extra juice. Push them gently but firmly into the top of the focaccia – either in neat lines or randomly, but in a single even layer.

8 Scatter over the sugar and **ask an adult to help you** transfer the tray to the preheated oven. Bake the bread for about 25 minutes. **Ask an adult to help you** test that the bread is ready; it should be golden and firm, and the base should sound hollow when it is tapped.

9 Serve warm or at room temperature.

This baked polenta makes a lovely main course for vegetarians, but is also nice served with meat as a change from potatoes. Alternatively, try it with the tomato sauce used for the tuna balls in the recipe on page 75.

baked polenta with cheese
polenta grigliata alla formaggio

1 litre well-flavoured
   vegetable stock
250 g instant polenta
100 g Parmesan,
   freshly grated
2 handfuls of baby spinach,
   torn
100 g butter, softened
100 g Taleggio cheese
sunflower oil, to grease
salt and black pepper
a baking tray
a pastry cutter (optional)
a large ovenproof dish

Serves 4

1 Pour the stock into a large, heavy saucepan, then **ask an adult to help you** turn on the heat. Leave the stock to heat up until it is bubbling nicely. Pour in the polenta in a steady stream, stirring quickly all the time with a large balloon whisk. Do it gently so that it doesn't splash. Cook the polenta for the time recommended on the packet you are using (some are quicker to cook than others).

2 When the polenta is cooked and thick, remove it from the heat and pop it on a heatproof work surface. Use an oven glove to hold the saucepan handle. Swap the whisk for a wooden spoon and stir in the Parmesan, spinach, a little pepper and half the butter. Have a little try (making sure it's not too hot first!) and see how it tastes. Add a little salt if you think it needs it.

3 Put a little sunflower oil on a piece of kitchen paper and wipe it over the baking tray to oil it.

4 **Ask an adult to help you** pour the mixture out onto the baking tray, then smooth it over with a palette knife. Leave it to cool and set.

5 **Ask an adult to help you** preheat the oven to 200°C (400°F) Gas 6.

6 Cut the polenta into circles using a pastry cutter or an upside-down glass and lay the circles in the ovenproof dish. **Ask an adult to help you** chop the cheese into little pieces, then dot the cheese evenly over the circles of polenta. Dot the remaining butter over too.

7 **Ask an adult to help you** bake the polenta in the preheated oven for about 15–20 minutes, until the cheese is melted and bubbling.

Polenta is very similar to semolina and makes a lovely pudding. You can serve this dessert as soon as it is cooked but I think it's lovely when left to set and baked with butter and sugar. Because you are using the zest of the orange, try to buy an unwaxed orange so that you don't end up eating waxy peel.

sweet polenta pudding
polenta dolce

600 ml whole milk
1 large unwaxed orange
300 g instant polenta
120 g caster sugar,
  plus 2 tablespoons
  for the topping
50 g mixed candied peel
100 g candied orange peel
100 g sultanas
50 g salted butter,
  plus 2 tablespoons
  for the topping
2 eggs
sunflower oil, to grease
single cream, to serve
a baking tray
a pastry cutter (optional)
a large ovenproof serving
  dish

Serves 4

1 Pour 600 ml water and the milk into a large saucepan and **ask an adult to help you** turn on the heat to medium. Bring it to the boil.

2 In the meantime, **ask an adult to help you** grate the orange zest (see Tip on page 24).

3 Pour the polenta in a steady stream into the saucepan with the water and milk, stirring quickly all the time with a large balloon whisk. Do it gently so that it doesn't splash. Cook the polenta for the time recommended on the packet.

4 When the polenta is cooked and thick, remove it from the heat and pop it on a heatproof work surface. Use an oven glove to hold the saucepan handle. Swap the whisk for a wooden spoon and stir in the sugar, peel, sultanas, grated orange zest and butter. Stir until everything is evenly mixed and the butter has melted and been absorbed.

5 **Ask an adult to help you** crack the eggs into a small bowl and beat them until smooth.

6 Stir them into the polenta until everything is well mixed.

7 Put a little sunflower oil on a piece of kitchen paper and wipe it over the baking tray to oil it.

8 **Ask an adult to help you** pour the mixture out onto the baking tray, then smooth it over with a palette knife. Leave it to cool and set.

9 When you are ready to cook the polenta, **ask an adult to help you** preheat the oven to 200°C (400°F) Gas 6.

10 Cut the polenta into circles using a pastry cutter or an upside-down glass and lay the circles in the ovenproof serving dish.

11 To make the topping, **ask an adult to help you** melt the remaining butter in a saucepan. Drizzle the melted butter and the remaining sugar over the top of the polenta circles.

12 **Ask an adult to help you** transfer the dish to the preheated oven and bake the polenta for about 15–20 minutes, until golden. Serve with single cream.

By now, I think you'll have got the idea about just how much the Italians love to sit around the table and eat and drink and chat together! They don't hang around waiting for their food though; they want to get into the all-important business of eating straightaway! So first the bread goes on the table, and then, probably hot on the heels, a selection of antipasti (which means 'before the meal') will follow. There are lots of different things that might be served – anything from a simple bowl of olives, a plate of salami or some nice cheeses, to more complicated fare.

This section includes some ideas for antipasti and simple lunches, as well as some tasty snacks for those rumbly tum times that might crop up now and again…

antipasti, easy lunches & snacks

tomato & bread soup
pappa al pomodoro

800 g ripe tomatoes
4 garlic cloves
200 g stale, country-style
  bread
50 ml olive oil, plus extra
  to drizzle
200 ml chicken or
  vegetable stock
6–7 fresh basil leaves, torn
salt and black pepper
freshly grated Parmesan,
  to serve

Serves 4

1 **Ask an adult to help you** make a little nick in each tomato with the point of a knife. Put the tomatoes into a large, heatproof bowl.

2 **Ask an adult to help you** boil the kettle and pour the boiling water over the tomatoes until they are covered. Leave them for 3–4 minutes.

3 In the meantime, **ask an adult to help you** peel the garlic cloves (see Tip on page 18) and cut them into thin slices, then cut the bread into small chunks.

4 After 3–4 minutes, the tomato skins should have started to curl away from the tomatoes. Carefully drain off the water, rinse them in cold water to cool them down a little and, when you're sure they're cool enough to handle, peel the skin away.

5 Put the skinned tomatoes on a chopping board and cut them in half. Give them a squeeze to remove the seeds, then chop the tomato flesh roughly. Put into a saucepan.

6 **Ask an adult to help you** cook the soup, because you will need to work at the hob all the way through the rest of the recipe.

7 Heat the olive oil in a frying pan and fry the bread chunks over medium heat for about 2–3 minutes, until light golden.

8 Stir in the tomatoes and garlic and cook for 5 minutes or so, until the tomatoes are starting to look a little sticky.

9 Pour in the stock and torn basil leaves and cook for about 20 minutes more, until the liquid has reduced and the soup is pulpy.

10 Have a little try of the soup and add a little salt and black pepper to taste. Stir well.

11 Remove the pan from the heat and leave to cool a little.

12 Serve with some olive oil drizzled over the top and freshly grated Parmesan sprinkled over too.

This soup is very popular in the Tuscany region of Italy, and if you like tomatoey things, you'll love it. You can serve it hot, or at room temperature. I like it at room temperature with a good drizzle of extra virgin olive oil over the top. If you can't get really good, juicy, ripe tomatoes, use two 400-g tins of cherry tomatoes, pop them in a sieve and rinse away the juice.

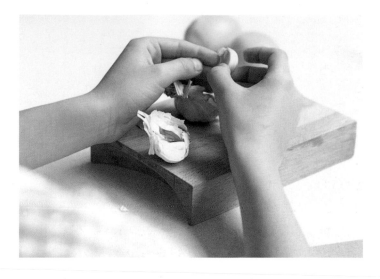

This is creamy and dreamy and you can make it with frozen peas, so it's quick as well as delicious!

creamy pea soup
crema di piselli

1 small onion
1 small potato (about 100 g)
1 garlic clove
3 tablespoons olive oil
700 g peas (fresh or frozen)
1 litre well-flavoured
   vegetable or chicken
   stock
3 tablespoons double cream
salt and black pepper
3 tablespoons olive oil,
   to drizzle
crusty bread, to serve

Serves 4

1 **Ask an adult to help you** prepare the vegetables. Peel the onion and chop it into fairly small pieces. Peel the potato and chop it into small, even-sized pieces. Peel the garlic clove (see Tip on page 18) and crush it with a garlic crusher.

2 **Ask an adult to help you** heat the olive oil in a large saucepan, then add the onion, garlic and potato. Cook over gentle heat for about 8–10 minutes, stirring quite often, until the onion is shiny and the potatoes are starting to soften.

3 Pour in the peas and the stock.

4 Leave the soup to simmer for about 20 minutes, until the potato is very soft – the potatoes should easily be squashed when you press them with a wooden spoon.

5 **Ask an adult to help you** remove the saucepan from the heat and liquidize the soup with a stick blender until it is smooth.

6 If you don't have a stick blender and are using a food processor or blender, you must let the soup cool a little before you blend it. Very hot soup can expand in the machine and may cause a nasty burn if you fill the machine too full.

7 Once the soup is nice and smooth, stir in the cream and season to taste with a little salt and some black pepper.

8 Spoon the mixture into pretty mugs or soup bowls, garnish with a drizzle of olive oil and serve with some good crusty bread.

These are crunchy and munchy and make a great snack if you're ravenous when you come in from school. Cut the bread diagonally, to give long, nicely shaped slices.

tomato toasts

crostini di pomodori

1 small ciabatta loaf
120 ml olive oil
4 ripe tomatoes
2 garlic cloves
a handful of fresh parsley
   leaves
salt and black pepper
2 baking trays

Serves 4

1 Ask an adult to help you preheat the oven to 200°C (400°F) Gas 6.

2 Ask an adult to help you cut the bread diagonally into thin slices. Put them on baking trays and drizzle them with a little olive oil. Bake in the preheated oven for 5–10 minutes, until crisp and golden.

3 In the meantime, **ask an adult to help you** slice the tomatoes in half and remove the core at the top. Chop the flesh roughly and put it into a bowl.

4 Peel the garlic cloves (see Tip on page 18), crush them with a garlic crusher, then put into the bowl with the tomatoes. Season with salt and black pepper and the remaining olive oil.

5 Ask an adult to help you chop the parsley leaves and stir into the bowl of tomatoes.

6 Ask an adult to help you remove the hot baking trays from the oven, then pile the mixture onto the toasts and serve.

These garlicky toasts make a great snack but you could also serve them alongside lots of other dishes. I think they taste much better than the usual garlic bread.

crispy garlic & olive oil toasts
fettunta

1 small ciabatta loaf
a handful of fresh parsley
  leaves
2–3 garlic cloves, halved
about 100 ml olive oil
rock salt
2 baking trays

Serves 4

1 **Ask an adult to help you** preheat the oven to 200°C (400°F) Gas 6.

2 **Ask an adult to help you** cut the bread diagonally into thin slices. Put them on baking trays and bake them in the preheated oven for 5 minutes, until crisp and golden.

3 In the meantime, **ask an adult to help you** chop the parsley leaves.

4 **Ask an adult to help you** remove the hot baking trays from the oven.

5 Rub the toasts all over with the cut surface of the garlic.

6 Drizzle a little olive oil over each toast, scatter over a tiny pinch of salt, sprinkle with the parsley and serve.

little savoury scones
bignè al formaggio

50 g butter
250 g self-raising flour
a pinch of salt
50 g Parmesan,
  freshly grated
150 ml milk
1 small egg

For the filling
1 celery stick
3–4 fresh chives
100 g squacquerone
  cheese
a pastry cutter (optional)
a baking tray
a pastry brush

Makes 8

More fillings to try
100 g soft cheese and
  2 slices of Parma ham,
  chopped
100 g hard cheese, grated,
  and 1 chopped tomato
2 boiled eggs, mashed and
  mixed with 1 teaspoon
  snipped fresh chives
a small tin of tuna in olive
  oil, drained and mixed
  with ½ small chopped
  onion and 1 small
  chopped tomato

1 **Ask an adult to help you** preheat the oven to 200°C (400°F) Gas 6.

2 **Ask an adult to help you** cut the butter into cubes. Put them in a bowl and sift over the flour and salt.

3 Put your hands in the bowl and rub the butter and flour together between your fingers and thumbs until the mixture looks like very fine breadcrumbs.

4 Stir in the Parmesan.

5 Start pouring in the milk, a little at a time. Keep mixing everything with your hands and adding milk until you have a soft but not sticky dough.

The Italians have a lovely soft cheese called squacquerone (pronounced skwok-er-o-nee), which is fabulously moreish and soft like the spreadable cheese you get in triangles here. If you can't find it, use cream cheese for this recipe instead, or choose your own favourite creamy cheese.

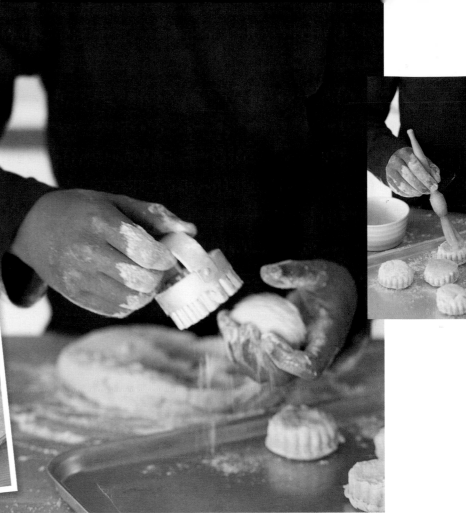

6 Sprinkle a little flour over a clean work surface and turn the dough out onto it. Using a rolling pin, roll it gently into a circle about 2 cm thick.

7 Cut the dough into rounds using a pastry cutter or a small, upside-down glass and lay the circles on a baking tray, leaving a little space between each.

8 Crack the egg into a small bowl, add 1 tablespoon water and beat lightly with a fork until it's well mixed. This is an egg wash.

9 Using a pastry brush, paint the tops of the scones with the egg wash. This will make the scones nice and glossy when they're baked.

10 Ask an adult to help you transfer the tray to the preheated oven and bake the scones for about 8–10 minutes, until they are firm and golden. Remove them and leave them to cool on a wire rack.

11 In the meantime, **ask an adult to help you** trim the ends of the celery and pull off some of the nasty stringy bits from the outside. Chop the celery finely. Snip the chives into pieces with kitchen scissors. Put the squacquerone cheese in a bowl and mix in the celery and chives.

12 Carefully cut the scones in half and spread some of the cheesy filling on each cut side.

little fried mozzarella & tomato sandwiches
mozzarella in carrozza

16 small, thin slices
   of bread
3–4 tomatoes
200 g mozzarella cheese,
   broken up into little
   pieces with your fingers
3 eggs
50 ml olive oil, to fry
salt and black pepper

Serves 4

1 **Ask an adult to help you** cut the crusts off the bread and thinly slice the tomatoes.

2 Dot the mozzarella over 8 of the bread slices and lay the slices of tomato over the top. Top with the remaining bread slices and press lightly to seal.

3 Crack the eggs into a bowl, then beat with a fork until they are nice and smooth. Pour them into a shallow container in which you can fit the sandwiches. Lay the sandwiches in the egg and leave them for 2–3 minutes to soak up the egg. Turn them over and leave them for another 2–3 minutes so that the other side is soaked in egg too.

4 **Ask an adult to help you** fry the sandwiches. You will more than likely have to cook them in at least 2 batches, depending on the size of the frying pan you have.

5 Heat a little of the olive oil in a non-stick frying pan and fry the sandwiches on one side for about 3 minutes, until the bread is golden. Carefully turn the sandwiches over and fry for a further 2–3 minutes, until that side is golden too; the cheese inside should be well melted.

6 **Ask an adult to help you** remove the sandwiches from the pan, cut them in half diagonally and serve them straightaway.

These are lovely because they are crisp and eggy on the outside and gooey and creamy on the inside. They are a popular snack all over Italy. Add slices of ham if you like.

Pinzimonio is often served in restaurants as a nibble while you are waiting for dinner but sometimes, if you're having a long, very rich meal, it's offered partway through to freshen the appetite. A variety of raw vegetables is served in a bowl over ice to keep it fresh, then everyone dips them into really delicious olive oil. It makes a refreshing alternative to heavier cream- or cheese-based dips. You must use a good extra virgin olive oil though!

little tomato cups with olive oil & crunchy vegetable dippers
pinzimonio in coppette di pomodoro

1 carrot
1 small celery stick
1 small red pepper
1 small yellow pepper
a small handful of fine
    green beans
4 vine-ripened tomatoes
80 ml olive oil
salt and black pepper

Serves 4

1 Wash all the vegetables well.

2 **Ask an adult to help you** prepare the vegetables. Top and tail the carrot and peel it with a vegetable peeler. Cut it into thin sticks or fingers, each about 4 cm long.

3 **Ask an adult to help you** trim the ends of the celery and pull off some of the nasty stringy bits from the outside. Cut it into pieces roughly the same size as the carrots.

4 Cut the red and yellow peppers in half, scrape out the seeds and remove the stalks. Cut the flesh into thin sticks or fingers too.

5 Top and tail the green beans and cut them in half to make them a similar size to the peppers and carrots.

6 To keep the vegetables fresh and crisp, pop them into a bowl of ice-cold water until you are ready to eat them.

7 Meanwhile, cut the tops carefully off the tomatoes. Using a teaspoon, scoop out the seeds and core of each tomato, taking care not to damage the sides of the tomato or make any holes. Make sure you leave it nice and clean inside.

8 Lay the tomatoes in the centre of a pretty platter and sprinkle the tiniest pinch of salt in each.

9 Carefully pour in enough olive oil to come two-thirds the way up the tomato cups.

10 Arrange the vegetable sticks nicely around the tomato cups and serve.

This recipe makes A LOT of breadsticks but the amount really depends how thick and how long you make them. Don't worry, they freeze very well and can be crisped up in the oven when required.

parmesan breadsticks
grissini con parmigiano

500 g strong bread flour,
   plus extra to sprinkle
1 sachet (7 g) fast action
   dried yeast
1 teaspoon salt
1 tablespoon olive oil
about 200 ml warm water
   (see Tip on page 30)
100 g Parmesan,
   freshly grated
2 large baking trays,
   dusted with flour

Makes ... oodles!

1 **Ask an adult to help you** preheat the oven to 220°C (425°F) Gas 7.

2 Put the flour, yeast and salt in a bowl and stir well. Stir in the olive oil and just 1–2 tablespoons warm water. Put your hands right in the bowl and mix the ingredients with your fingers. Keep adding warm water, a little at a time, until you have a soft but not sticky dough.

3 Scatter the Parmesan over the bread and knead well, until all the cheese has been mixed into the dough.

4 Sprinkle a little flour over a clean work surface, turn the dough out onto it and knead for 5–10 minutes (see Tip on page 13). The dough should be very smooth and elastic.

5 Break off pieces of dough about the size of large walnuts and roll into long sticks using your hands. Lay the breadsticks on the prepared baking trays.

6 **Ask an adult to help you** put the breadsticks into the preheated oven and bake for about 5 minutes, until golden and crisp. Remove from the oven and leave to cool on wire racks.

Almost as soon as you sit down in a restaurant in Italy, you'll be offered bread, shortly followed by a plate of scrumptious things to nibble on and get your appetite going for what's to come. All these nibbles are called antipasti. If you're planning to make a special meal, an antipasti platter is an easy way to serve a starter and it's especially nice because it's very relaxed – you can make it well ahead of time, and then when the meal starts, you can just let everyone chat away and help themselves. Take a pretty platter and build a selection from the following ideas.

antipasti platter

ITALIAN MEATS

The Italians make a lot of different cured meats ('cured' means that they are preserved by marinating in herbs or spices and then dried in the mountain air for a long time to preserve them, rather than being cooked). Some typical kinds are salami (cured pork with spices), Parma ham (cured pork from Parma in northern Italy), speck (another kind of cured pork), San Daniele ham (similar to Parma ham) and bresaola (very thin slices of cured beef).

BREADSTICKS WITH PARMA HAM

Make a batch of the breadsticks on the page opposite. Buy some Parma ham and cut the slices into 3 strips. Wrap a strip around the top of each breadstick.

SUN-DRIED TOMATOES ON STICKS

Buy sun-dried tomatoes preserved in olive oil and drain them, then spear them onto cocktail sticks. They're especially good if you add a little cube of crumbly cheese, such as Parmesan, or even tiny little balls of mozzarella called bocconcini (see right).

SLICES OF ITALIAN CHEESE

If you have a good local deli or your supermarket has a good cheese counter, have a look for Italian cheeses such as Provolone, Asiago, Fontina or pecorino, although you could cheat and use some cheeses from other countries too! All you need to do is slice them thinly and arrange them in an attractive way on a pretty platter.

LITTLE NUGGETS OF PARMESAN

All you have to do is carefully dig out little nuggets of Parmesan with a knife and spear them with cocktail sticks, ready for picking up.

BOCCONCINI

Bocconcini are little bite-sized balls of mozzarella cheese. Add a little pile to your platter and put some cocktail sticks nearby.

OLIVES

Choose green olives if you like them tangy and firm and black if you prefer them softer and oilier. Even if you're not keen on them at all, keep trying – you might grow to like them. And don't forget that your guests might love them!

Although in modern Italy meals no longer involve quite as many courses as they would in days gone by (unless it's a particular time of the year such as Christmas or a special celebration), very often in Italy you can expect to eat as much as an antipasti course, followed by a bowl of pasta and then a meat or fish dish as a main course – not forgetting dessert at the end. Of course, you could do the same and serve the dishes in the following section after two courses and before the sweet, but you might like to serve slightly smaller portions! In any case, there is a good selection to suit either a weekday meal or a special occasion to impress family and friends.

main courses

This is really easy and tasty. It goes really well with the tomato sauce on page 75 and the rosemary potatoes on page 82.

meatloaf
polpettone

1 onion
2 garlic cloves
1 egg
900 g lean minced beef
2 teaspoons dried oregano
150 g Parmesan,
    freshly grated
salt and black pepper
Tomato Sauce (page 75),
    to serve
Rosemary Potatoes
    (page 82), to serve
a 450-g loaf tin

Serves 4

1 Put the loaf tin on a sheet of greaseproof paper and draw around the base. Cut out the rectangle and lay it in the bottom of the tin to line it.

2 **Ask an adult to help you** preheat the oven to 180°C (350°F) Gas 4.

3 **Ask an adult to help you** peel and chop the onion into quite small pieces. Peel the garlic cloves (see Tip on page 18) and crush them with a garlic crusher. Put the onion and garlic into a large bowl.

4 Crack the egg into a bowl and beat with a fork until smooth. Pour into the bowl with the onion and garlic along with the minced beef, oregano and Parmesan.

5 Season well with salt and black pepper.

6 Put your hands right in the bowl and mix the ingredients with your fingers until everything is well combined.

7 Spoon the mixture into the loaf tin and smooth the top with the back of a spoon.

8 **Ask an adult to help you** transfer the tin to the preheated oven and cook for 45 minutes.

9 **Ask an adult to help you** remove the tin from the oven and turn the meatloaf out onto a chopping board. Cut in slices and serve with Tomato Sauce and Rosemary Potatoes.

cheat's pea, sausage & onion calzone
calzone con piselli, salsiccia e cipolla

250 g good-quality
   sausages
1 onion
2 garlic cloves
2 ripe tomatoes
6 tablespoons olive oil
150 g frozen peas,
   defrosted
4 small flour tortillas
3 tablespoons mascarpone
1 small egg
salt and black pepper
a pastry brush

Serves 4

1 **Ask an adult to help you** cut away the skins of the sausages with kitchen scissors and throw the skins away. Pull the sausagemeat into chunks, put in a bowl and set aside.

2 **Ask an adult to help you** peel the onion and chop it finely. Peel the garlic cloves (see Tip on page 18) and crush them with a garlic crusher.

3 **Ask an adult to help you** slice the top off the tomatoes and squeeze out the seeds. Chop the flesh into small pieces.

4 **Ask an adult to help you** heat 3 tablespoons of the olive oil in a saucepan and fry the onion and garlic over gentle heat for 3–4 minutes, until the onion is starting to soften.

5 Add the sausagemeat and season with salt and black pepper. Cook for 1–2 minutes longer, until the sausagemeat is golden. Give it all a good stir every once in a while.

6 Add the tomatoes and peas to the pan. Stir well and cook for another 15 minutes or so, until all the liquid has disappeared, the meat is cooked and the mixture is deliciously sticky.

7 Lay the tortillas out on a chopping board and spoon one-quarter of the mixture onto one side of each tortilla, leaving a 2-cm border around the edges. Dot little bits of mascarpone over the sausagemeat mixture.

8 Crack the egg into a bowl and beat with a fork until smooth.

9 Brush some beaten egg around the edge of the tortillas with a pastry brush. Fold over each tortilla to make a semi-circle shape. Press the edges down to seal them.

10 **Ask an adult to help you** heat the remaining oil in a large frying pan over medium heat and fry the tortillas for 3–4 minutes on each side, until golden. Drain on kitchen paper.

Calzone are a bit like pasties made from pizza dough. Although in my recipe they are made with tortillas, they taste every bit as good and are lighter and quicker to make.

There isn't much to say about this easy-peasy tart — it's just too delicious for words!

upside-down cheese & tomato tart
sfogliata al formaggio e pomodoro

½ slice of stale white bread
150 g Provolone cheese
400 g cherry tomatoes
2 tablespoons olive oil,
   plus extra to grease
plain flour, to sprinkle
300 g puff pastry,
   defrosted if frozen
salt and black pepper
a crisp, green salad,
   to serve
a 23-cm loose-bottomed
   tart tin

Serves 4

1 **Ask an adult to help you** preheat the oven to 200°C (400°F) Gas 6.

2 Put a little olive oil on a piece of kitchen paper and wipe the base of the tart tin with it to oil it.

3 **Ask an adult to help you** whiz the bread in a food processor until you get crumbs. Scatter over the bottom of the tart tin.

4 **Ask an adult to help you** cut the cheese into small, thin slices and arrange them over the breadcrumbs. Scatter the tomatoes over the cheese slices, drizzle with the olive oil and season with salt and black pepper.

5 Sprinkle a little flour over a clean work surface and put the puff pastry on it. Using a rolling pin, roll it gently into a circle slightly larger than the tart tin.

6 Lay the pastry over the tomatoes and tuck the edges into the tin.

7 **Ask an adult to help you** put the tart into the preheated oven and bake for about 25 minutes, until the pastry is golden brown and risen.

8 **Ask an adult to help you** remove the tart from the oven and leave it to cool for about 5 minutes, until it is cool enough to handle safely with oven gloves on.

9 **Ask an adult to help you** place an upturned dinner plate (larger than the tart tin) over the tin. Carefully flip everything over so that the plate is on the bottom. Pull the tin away and the tart should slip out onto the plate. The tomatoes will be on top now and the cheese should be lovely and melted. Serve in slices, with a crisp, green salad.

67

salmon on sticks
spiedini di salmone

600 g salmon fillet
a small bunch of fresh
   chives
freshly squeezed juice of
   ½ small lemon
salt
450 g cherry tomatoes
3 tablespoons olive oil
lemon wedges, to serve
Tomato & Bread Salad
   (page 89), to serve
   (optional)
12 wooden skewers,
   about 30 cm long
a ridged griddle pan
a pastry brush

Makes about 12

1 Soak the skewers in a dish of cold water for 30 minutes. This will stop them burning when you put them on the hot griddle pan.

2 Meanwhile, **ask an adult to help you** cut the salmon into bite-sized chunks. Snip the chives into pieces with kitchen scissors.

3 Pop the salmon, lemon juice and chives in a large bowl and season with a little salt.

4 Push a chunk of salmon onto a skewer and then a tomato. Continue pushing alternate pieces of salmon and tomato onto skewers until you run out of salmon and tomatoes (leave 6 cm clear at each end of the skewers).

5 **Ask an adult to help you** heat a ridged griddle pan until quite hot. Brush the olive oil over the skewers with a pastry brush. Lay them on the hot griddle pan and cook for about 5–6 minutes, until the salmon is cooked through and golden brown. Turn them over once halfway through cooking. You will need to cook them in batches.

6 Serve with lemon wedges to squeeze over. You might like to try it with the Tomato & Bread Salad.

Spiedini are very popular in Italy – they are skewers of meat or fish and vegetables, very similar to kebabs. These salmon spiedini are especially tasty cooked on the barbecue in the summer, but you can cook them just as easily on a griddle pan too.

Arrosticini are very famous in the area of Italy where I live – they even have special grills to cook them on that look like long, thin trough-shaped barbecues. Arrosticini are made from tiny cubes of mutton threaded onto skewers and the special grill is designed so that the ends of the skewers don't sit over the heat and burn. For this recipe, I've used little squares of lamb, and with some adult help, you can easily cook them on a griddle pan or barbecue – they're incredibly easy to make and far too tasty not to try!

abruzzese-style lamb skewers
arrosticini

500 g lamb fillet
salt
tomato salad, to serve
Rosemary Potatoes
    (page 82), to serve
30 wooden skewers,
    about 30 cm long

Makes about 30

1 Soak the skewers in a dish of cold water for 30 minutes. This will stop them burning when you put them on the hot griddle pan.

2 Meanwhile, **ask an adult to help you** cut the lamb into small bite-sized chunks.

3 Push the pieces of lamb onto the skewers until you run out of lamb (leave 6 cm clear at each end of the skewers).

4 Season the lamb with salt.

5 **Ask an adult to help you** heat a ridged griddle pan until quite hot. Lay the skewers on the pan and cook for about 10 minutes, until the lamb is cooked through and dark brown. Turn them over once halfway through cooking. You will need to cook them in batches.

6 Serve with a tomato salad and some Rosemary Potatoes.

Frittatas are eaten all over Italy. They're a little bit like flat omelettes. They're often cooked on the cooker and finished off under the grill, but this one is easier because it's simply baked in the oven. It's made with pieces of Italian bacon (pancetta lardons, see page 9) and sweet leeks, but you could try other vegetables – courgettes, onions, mushrooms, peas, tomatoes, beans – and even add your favourite grated cheese too.

leek frittata
frittata con porri

3 leeks
100 g pancetta lardons
2 tablespoons olive oil
8 large eggs
a few fresh chives
salt and black pepper
a crisp, green salad,
   to serve
*a round ovenproof dish
   with a diameter of about
   23 cm*

Serves 4

1 Ask an adult to help you preheat the oven to 200°C (400°F) Gas 6.

2 Ask an adult to help you trim off the bottom of the leeks and cut off any thick, dark leaves at the top. Cut the leeks in half along their length and wash them very well – sometimes grit can get caught between the leaves.

3 Cut the leeks into fine slices and scatter them over the base of the ovenproof dish.

4 Scatter over the pancetta lardons and drizzle with the olive oil.

5 Ask an adult to help you pop the dish in the preheated oven and roast for about 15 minutes, until the pancetta is cooked and the leeks are softened.

6 In the meantime, crack the eggs into a bowl and beat with a balloon whisk until very smooth. Season with salt and black pepper.

7 Ask an adult to help you remove the hot dish from the oven and put it on a heatproof surface. Carefully pour in the eggs, taking care not to touch the hot dish.

8 Snip the chives into pieces with kitchen scissors and scatter over the frittata.

9 Ask an adult to help you return the dish to the oven and bake for about 20 minutes longer, until the eggs are set.

10 Ask an adult to help you take the dish out of the oven. Serve with a crisp, green salad. You can serve it warm or cold, if you prefer.

These tasty little fish balls are so simple to make and the great thing is that everything you need can probably be found in your kitchen cupboard, making them a brilliant standby if you have unexpected visitors for lunch! Try to use tuna preserved in olive oil, or at the very least in sunflower oil – it's tastier, has a better texture and is much healthier than the tinned tuna in brine.

74

cheese & tuna fish balls
with tomato sauce
polpettine al tonno con salsa di pomodoro

4–5 tablespoons olive oil
salt and black pepper

For the tuna fish balls
2 thick slices of white
  bread, crusts removed
two 250-g tins tuna in olive
  oil, drained
1 egg
150 g mature Cheddar,
  grated

For the tomato sauce
1 onion
2 garlic cloves
3 tablespoons olive oil
400-g tin tomatoes
2 teaspoons caster sugar
a small handful of fresh
  basil leaves, torn (or ½
  teaspoon dried oregano)

Serves 4

1 To make the tuna fish balls, **ask an adult to help you** cut the crusts off the bread and whiz the bread in a food processor until you get crumbs. Transfer the breadcrumbs to a bowl with the tuna and stir until well mixed.

2 Crack the egg into the bowl, then add the cheese. Season with salt and black pepper.

3 Take a small amount of the tuna mixture in your hands and roll it around between your palms to make a walnut-sized ball. Repeat with the rest of the mixture until there is none left. Set the fish balls aside.

4 To make the tomato sauce, **ask an adult to help you** peel the onion and chop it finely. Peel the garlic cloves (see Tip on page 18) and crush them with a garlic crusher.

5 **Ask an adult to help you** heat the olive oil in a saucepan and fry the onion and garlic over gentle heat for 4–5 minutes, until the onion has softened but not coloured.

6 Add the tinned tomatoes and sugar to the pan and season with a little salt and black pepper. Leave the sauce to bubble for about 10–15 minutes, until glossy and thick, then add the basil and leave the mixture to simmer gently for 5 minutes more.

7 **Ask an adult to help you** heat the olive oil in a frying pan and fry the fish balls for about 4–5 minutes, until hot and golden. Transfer them to a dish and pour the tomato sauce over the top. Serve with pasta or potatoes and vegetables.

The Italians make fabulously meaty sausages and one of my favourites is called luganega. If you can't find these, just use good-quality pork sausages. Don't worry about the whole cloves of garlic in this – when cooked this way, garlic is mild and delicious squashed onto the bread with the beans when you're eating it.

sausage & beans
salsicce con fagioli

2 red onions

12 good-quality sausages

3 tablespoons olive oil

4–5 garlic cloves

two 400-g tins cherry tomatoes, drained and rinsed

250 ml good vegetable or meat stock

1 dried bay leaf

400-g tin cannellini beans, drained and rinsed

a small handful of fresh parsley leaves

4 slices of country-style bread, toasted, to serve

an ovenproof casserole dish or deep roasting tin

Serves 4

1 **Ask an adult to help you** preheat the oven to 200°C (400°F) Gas 6.

2 **Ask an adult to help you** peel the onions, cut them in half and slice each half thinly. Scatter them over the base of the ovenproof casserole dish or deep roasting tin.

3 Scatter the sausages over the onions and drizzle everything with the olive oil.

4 **Ask an adult to help you** transfer the dish to the preheated oven and roast for about 20 minutes, until the onions are soft and the sausages have started to colour.

5 **Ask an adult to help you** take the dish out of the oven.

6 Peel the garlic cloves (see Tip on page 18) and scatter them whole over the sausages in the dish.

7 Add the tinned tomatoes, stock, bay leaf and beans. **Ask an adult to help you** return the dish to the oven. Bake for 30 minutes longer, until the onions are tender and the sausages are cooked through.

8 **Ask an adult to help you** remove the dish from the oven and chop the parsley leaves. Stir in all but a spoonful of the parsley.

9 Put a slice of bread in each of 4 bowls. Spoon the sausages and beans over the bread, and some of the sauce around. Scatter the remaining parsley over the top.

This dish doesn't make the prettiest sauce you'll ever come across but it may well be one of the tastiest! The chicken ends up fabulously juicy, and the milk and lemons bubble down to make sticky, citrussy nuggets. Tell everyone to squash the soft garlic out of its skin and smear it onto the meat too!

chicken poached in milk & lemons
pollo con latte e limone

2 small, unwaxed lemons
a 2.5-kg chicken
30 ml olive oil
1 whole garlic bulb,
    cloves separated but
    left unpeeled
a small bunch of fresh sage
1 litre whole milk
salt and black pepper
bread, to serve

Serves 6

1 Ask an adult to help you cut each lemon into 6 wedges.

2 Season the chicken. **Ask an adult to help you** heat half the olive oil in a large saucepan and cook the chicken, breast-side down, for 4–5 minutes, until golden. Turn the chicken over and cook for 3–4 minutes more.

3 Ask an adult to help you remove the chicken from the pan and pour away any used oil.

4 Pour the remaining olive oil into the pan and add the lemon wedges and garlic. Stir-fry for 2–3 minutes, until golden. Add the sage and cook for another minute or so.

5 Return the chicken to the pan and pour the milk over it.

6 Put a lid on the pan, leaving a little opening to allow for the steam to escape. Simmer over gentle heat for about 1 hour, until the meat is cooked through and the sauce has curdled into sticky nuggets (take care to keep the heat low, or the milk will reduce too quickly to fully cook the chicken).

7 Ask an adult to help you remove the pan from the heat. Leave the chicken to rest for 4–5 minutes before slicing. Serve warm with the sauce and bread to mop up the sauce.

On the whole, Italians don't tend to serve a huge range of vegetables alongside the main course – perhaps just one vegetable such as potatoes or maybe a salad and occasionally both. But they do have a wonderful way with them. Here is a selection of vegetables that should be easy to find anywhere. I hope these recipes will prove to you that vegetables don't have to be boring and that there's more to salad than just lettuce and tomatoes!

vegetables & salads

Potatoes roasted with rosemary and garlic are heavenly.
They are the perfect accompaniment to a Sunday roast.

rosemary potatoes
patate con rosmarino

1 kg floury potatoes
  (such as Maris Piper
  or King Edward)
4 tablespoons olive oil
2 garlic cloves
a small handful of fresh
  rosemary leaves
salt and black pepper

Serves 4

1 Ask an adult to help you preheat the oven to 200° C (400°F) Gas 6.

2 Ask an adult to help you peel the potatoes and cut them into small chunks. Put them in a bowl, cover with water and leave them to soak for 10 minutes, then drain and pat dry with kitchen paper.

3 Pour the olive oil into a roasting tin and **ask an adult to help you** put it in the preheated oven. Heat for 3–4 minutes until the oil is hot.

4 Peel the garlic cloves (see Tip on page 18) and crush them with a garlic crusher.

5 Ask an adult to help you to remove the tin from the oven and carefully add the potatoes, taking care that the hot oil doesn't splash. Return the tin to the oven and roast the potatoes for about 35 minutes, until crisp and golden and almost soft.

6 Ask an adult to help you chop the rosemary.

7 Ask an adult to help you remove the tin from the oven and scatter the garlic, rosemary and some salt and black pepper over the potatoes. Stir and return to the oven for 5–10 minutes longer. Drain the potatoes on kitchen paper before serving.

Broccoli is fine by itself, but don't you think it can seem a little bit boring sometimes? Well, try it the way the Italians often serve it, with a drizzle of olive oil and a scattering of crispy crumbs. Once upon a time, fried crumbs like this were used by peasants as a substitute for Parmesan cheese, because Parmesan was very expensive and the crumbs added a similar texture; now people just add the breadcrumbs anyway because they taste so good!

broccoli with poor man's parmesan
broccolo con aglio e muddica

600 g broccoli

Poor man's parmesan
2 garlic cloves
1 unwaxed lemon
2 tablespoons fresh parsley leaves
5–6 slices of white bread
4 tablespoons olive oil
salt and black pepper

Serves 4

1 Break the broccoli into small florets and put into a saucepan. Pour in enough water to cover the broccoli.

2 Ask an adult to help you put the pan on the hob over quite high heat. Bring to the boil.

3 Turn the heat down and simmer until the broccoli is almost soft but still has a little bite to it. **Ask an adult to help you** test it by pricking it gently with the tip of a sharp knife – it should feel quite soft but not so soft that it slips off the knife.

4 Ask an adult to help you drain the broccoli and transfer it to a dish to keep warm while you make the poor man's Parmesan.

5 Peel the garlic cloves (see Tip on page 18) and crush them with a garlic crusher.

6 Wash the lemon and **ask an adult to help you** grate the zest (see Tip on page 24) and to chop the parsley.

7 Ask an adult to help you whiz the bread in a food processor until you get crumbs. Transfer to a large bowl and stir in the garlic, lemon zest, parsley and a little salt and black pepper.

8 Ask an adult to help you heat 2 tablespoons of the olive oil in a frying pan and add the crumb mixture. Cook over gentle heat for 2–3 minutes, until crisp and golden.

9 Drizzle over the remaining olive oil and scatter over the poor man's Parmesan.

Strictly speaking, Italians aren't big dessert eaters (it's hardly surprising when you think how many other courses there might be during one meal!) Desserts to follow lunch or dinner will very often consist of seasonal fruit, which isn't a bad thing at all considering the wonderful choice on offer throughout most of the year. They do make some great cakes and pastries, but these might be eaten at breakfast time or with coffee in the morning. Here are some of my favourites, and of course, you can choose to eat them at any time of the day!

One dessert the Italians are big fans of is ice cream – and they really do make the dreamiest ice cream. It takes real willpower to walk past a gelateria (ice-cream shop) on a hot summer's day without calling in to buy a cone of their irresistible, irresistible, velvety-smooth gelato. The flavours available are out of this world. I realize that unless you're super lucky, hopping over to Italy just for an ice cream isn't very likely to be possible, so here are some lip-licking recipes that will let an Italian ice cream come to you!

sweets & ice cream

We buy moist little coconut cakes like this in our local pastry shop. They make a lovely sweet treat.

coconut kisses
baci di cocco

50 g butter, plus extra
  to grease
200 g desiccated coconut
50 g caster sugar
1 egg
a baking tray

Makes about 10

1 Ask an adult to help you preheat the oven to 150°C (300°C) Gas 2. Put a little butter on a piece of kitchen paper and rub it over the baking tray to grease it.

2 Ask an adult to help you melt the butter in a small saucepan, then leave it to cool for a while.

3 Put the coconut, sugar and butter in a large bowl and stir until well mixed.

4 Crack the egg into a separate bowl and beat with a fork, then add to the other ingredients and stir well.

5 Take walnut-sized amounts of the mixture in your hands and shape into small pyramids. Put on the baking tray and ask an adult to help you transfer them to the oven. Bake for 15 minutes or so, until golden.

6 Transfer to a wire rack and leave to cool.

This is the sort of quick dessert that Italian children might have if their mums are busy – just as we might have a carton of yoghurt for pudding sometimes. Stir a pinch of ground cinnamon into the sugar if you like.

sugared ricotta with fresh fruit

500 g chilled ricotta
2–3 tablespoons caster
  sugar
fresh fruit, to serve

Serves 4

1 Spoon the ricotta into dessert bowls and sprinkle the sugar over the top.

2 Serve with your favourite fresh fruit.

Delicious pancake parcels oozing with sweet, sticky mascarpone, honey and pears – yum!

baked pancake parcels with pears & mascarpone

crespelle di pere e mascarpone

30 g butter, plus extra to grease

For the pancakes
30 g butter
2 eggs
300 ml milk
a pinch of salt
120 g plain flour, sifted

For the filling
500 g mascarpone
3 ripe but firm pears
4 tablespoons dark runny honey (chestnut, if possible)
an ovenproof dish

Serves 4

1 To make the pancakes, **ask an adult to help you** melt the butter in a pan, then pour it into the bowl of a food processor or in a blender with the eggs and milk and whiz to combine.

2 Sift the salt and flour into the bowl and whiz until you have a smooth batter. Set aside for 30 minutes–1 hour.

3 **Ask an adult to help you** cook the pancakes. Put a little of the butter for frying in a small non-stick frying pan or crêpe pan and heat over medium heat until hot. If the batter has thickened, you may need to add a little water.

4 Pour in a small amount of batter (just enough to cover the base of the frying pan) and tilt the pan to spread the mixture evenly. Cook for 1–2 minutes, until the pancake is golden on the underside and little bubbles have started to appear on the surface. Using a palette knife, loosen the pancake around the edges and turn it over. Cook for another minute, until golden brown.

5 Repeat until all the remaining batter has been used up – it should make 8 pancakes. Keep adding butter a little at a time between pancakes to keep the frying pan greased.

6 Put the finished pancakes on top of a large sheet of aluminium foil and stack them between layers of greaseproof paper. Wrap up the foil and put the parcel in a low oven until you are ready to use the pancakes.

7 To make the filling, put the mascarpone in a large bowl and beat until smooth, then remove 3 tablespoons to another small bowl.

8 **Ask an adult to help you** peel the pears, remove the cores and cut the flesh into small pieces. Fold lightly into the large bowl of mascarpone. Fold in 2 tablespoons of the honey very lightly to give a rippled effect.

9 **Ask an adult to help you** preheat the grill until hot. Put a little butter on a piece of kitchen paper and rub it over the ovenproof dish to grease it. Remove the pancakes from the oven and lay one out flat on a chopping board. Spoon an eighth of the pear mixture onto the centre. Fold into a flat parcel and put in the dish, seam-side down. Repeat with the remaining pancakes.

10 Dot the remaining mascarpone over the parcels and drizzle over the last of the honey. Grill for 4 minutes until golden and bubbling.

Italian children love these pretty filled biscuits; they usually come filled with jam or chocolate. I usually make some of each!

little filled flower biscuits

90 g butter, softened
60 g icing sugar
1 egg yolk
150 g Italian type 'oo' flour,
   plus extra to sprinkle
jam or chocolate spread,
   to fill
icing sugar, to dust
2 baking trays
2 pastry cutters, 5 cm and
   1 cm

Makes 10

1 **Ask an adult to help you** preheat the oven to 180°C (350°F) Gas 4. Line the baking trays with greaseproof paper.

2 Put the butter and sugar into a bowl and beat with a wooden spoon until smooth.

3 Add the egg yolk and beat again until it is well mixed in.

4 Stir in the flour and mix until you get a soft but not sticky dough.

5 Sprinkle a little flour over a clean work surface, turn the dough out onto it and roll out with a rolling pin until it is about 2 mm thick. Using the larger pastry cutter, stamp out rounds from the dough.

6 Take the smaller pastry cutter or a small upside-down glass and cut out a small hole in the centre of half the large rounds. Remove

the centre pieces; the biscuits with the holes will make the tops. Gather up the leftover trimmings and reroll them to make more circles until all the pastry is used up.

7 Lay the circles on the prepared baking trays.

8 **Ask an adult to help you** transfer the trays to the preheated oven and bake the biscuits for about 6–8 minutes, until crisp and light golden. Remove the tray from the oven and leave them to cool.

9 When the biscuits are cold, spread a little jam or chocolate spread over one of the complete rounds and place one of the biscuits with the holes on top. Repeat with the remaining biscuits, then dust with a little icing sugar. Store in an airtight tin until ready to serve.

80 g dark chocolate

For the pastry
175 g butter, softened
75 g caster sugar
1 egg yolk
250 g plain flour, plus extra
   to sprinkle

For the filling
250 g mascarpone cheese
2 tablespoons caster sugar
1 kg mixed summer berries
   (such as strawberries,
   raspberries and
   blueberries)
*a 23-cm loose-bottomed
   tart tin*
a pastry brush

Serves 6

This is a beautiful tart to make for a party; it looks just like the ones you find in lovely Italian pastry shops. A slice of this is like a little bit of summer sunshine on your plate! Glazing the case with chocolate means you can fill the case with the fruit ahead of time without the pastry going soggy.

summer fruit tart
crostata di frutta d'estate

1 To make the pastry, put the butter and sugar into a bowl and beat with a wooden spoon until smooth.

2 Add the egg yolk and beat again until it is well mixed in.

3 Stir in the flour and mix until you get a soft but not sticky dough.

4 Divide the dough in half. Put half into a plastic bag and freeze it to use next time.

5 Sprinkle a little flour over a clean work surface, turn the dough out onto it and roll out with a rolling pin until it is just a little bit bigger than the tart tin.

6 Sprinkle a little flour over the rolling pin to stop it being sticky. Roll the pastry over the rolling pin, lift it all up and carefully unroll it over the tart tin.

7 Press the pastry gently into the corners and repair any holes with a little extra pastry.

8 Trim the edges so that the pastry case is nice and neat, then pop it into the fridge for 30 minutes or so, to firm up.

9 **Ask an adult to help you** preheat the oven to 180°C (350°F) Gas 4.

10 Take the tart tin out of the fridge and transfer to the preheated oven. Bake for 10–15 minutes, until crisp and golden. Remove from the oven and leave to cool.

11 Break the chocolate up into pieces and pop it in a small heatproof bowl. **Ask an adult to help you** set the bowl over a saucepan of gently simmering water, making sure that the bottom of the bowl does not touch the water. Stir the chocolate with a wooden spoon until it has melted. Take it off the heat and leave it to cool for a while.

12 Using a pastry brush, paint the base of the pastry with the melted chocolate and leave it to set.

13 To make the filling, put the mascarpone and sugar in a bowl and beat until smooth. Spoon it into the tart case.

14 Scatter the berries evenly over the mascarpone and serve in slices.

The Italians often add almonds to their cakes and it helps to create a wonderfully dense, moist cake. They also like using polenta in cakes – and luckily polenta is now very easy to find in the supermarkets, but dried semolina makes a good substitute if necessary. I think this cake is perfect served as a dessert with some fresh fruit but quite a few of the children I know seem to love it with a glass of milk as an afternoon treat and adults seem to enjoy a slice with a cuppa too!

almond cake
torta alle mandorle

250 g butter, softened, plus extra to grease

250 g caster sugar

4 large eggs, cracked into a bowl

200 g ground almonds

100 g polenta

50 g self-raising flour

1 unwaxed lemon

icing sugar, to dust

a 23-cm springform cake tin

Serves 10

1 Ask an adult to help you preheat the oven to 150°C (300°F) Gas 2.

2 Put a little butter on a piece of kitchen paper and rub it over the cake tin to grease it. Take the bottom out of the cake tin, lay it on a sheet of greaseproof paper and draw around it. Cut out the circle. Put the cake tin back together and lay the paper circle in the bottom of the tin to line it.

3 Ask an adult to help you beat the butter and sugar together in a large bowl with an electric whisk until smooth, light and fluffy.

4 Add the eggs, a little at a time, stirring well between each addition.

5 Stir in the almonds, polenta and flour.

6 Wash the lemon and **ask an adult to help you** grate the zest (see Tip on page 24). Stir the zest into the bowl and squeeze in the juice from the lemon too.

7 Spoon the mixture evenly into the cake tin. **Ask an adult to help you** transfer the tin to the preheated oven and bake for 45 minutes or so, until the cake has risen and is golden and springy to the touch.

8 Ask an adult to help you remove the cake from the oven and leave to cool in the tin for 20 minutes or so, then turn out onto a wire rack to cool completely. Dust with icing sugar.

These make an indulgent treat for a special breakfast or a funky dessert with ice cream when your friends come around to eat!

fried chocolate sandwiches
sandwich croccanti con cioccolato

16 small, thin slices
  of bread
100 g mascarpone
80 g dark chocolate, grated
60 g butter

Serves 4

1 Cut the crusts off the bread and spread 8 of the slices with a thin layer of mascarpone.

2 Grate the chocolate with a cheese grater – mind those fingers! – and scatter a nice layer of it over the mascarpone. Put a plain slice of bread on top and press down lightly.

3 **Ask an adult to help you** melt a little butter in a non-stick frying pan and fry the sandwiches for about 3 minutes, until the

bread is golden and the chocolate is melting (You will have to cook the sandwiches in batches, depending on how big your frying pan is.)

4 Carefully turn the sandwiches over and fry for a further 2–3 minutes.

5 **Ask an adult to help you** remove the sandwiches from the pan and cut them in half diagonally. Eat them warm.

This looks every bit as delicious as it tastes. It makes a scrumptious dessert with some ice cream, but is also good for tucking into a lunchbox or picnic hamper.

apple cake
torta di mele

150 g butter, plus extra
   to grease
150 g caster sugar
2 eggs, cracked into a bowl
150 g ground almonds
50 g plain flour
1 teaspoon baking powder
1 unwaxed lemon
100 ml whole milk
2 red apples
icing sugar, to dust
a 450-g loaf tin

Serves 8–10

1 **Ask an adult to help you** preheat the oven to 150°C (300°F) Gas 2.

2 **Ask an adult to help you** melt the butter in a small pan.

3 Put a little butter on a piece of kitchen paper and rub it over the loaf tin to grease it. Put the tin on a sheet of greaseproof paper and draw around the base. Cut out the rectangle and lay it in the bottom of the tin to line it.

4 **Ask an adult to help you** beat the butter and sugar together in a large bowl with an electric whisk until smooth, light and fluffy.

5 Add the eggs, a little at a time, stirring well between each addition.

6 Stir in the almonds, flour and baking powder.

7 Wash the lemon and **ask an adult to help you** grate the zest (see Tip on page 24). Stir the zest into the bowl along with the milk.

8 Spoon the mixture evenly into the loaf tin.

9 **Ask an adult to help you** cut the apples in half. Remove the cores and cut the flesh into thin slices. Arrange evenly over the cake.

10 **Ask an adult to help you** transfer the tin to the preheated oven and bake for 45 minutes or so, until the cake has risen and is golden and springy to the touch. Remove the cake from the oven and leave to cool in the tin for 20 minutes, then turn out onto a wire rack to cool completely. Dust with icing sugar.

index